Love's Longings...

...leaving hearts on my canvas...

Third Edition

Written by

Carl Porten

Mage Orange

PUBLISHERS

Love's Longings...
...leaving hearts on my canvas...
Third Edition

ISBN: 978-81-949451-7-8

3rd Edition Published in 2022 by
Mage Orange Publishers
An imprint of Mage Orange Publication & Technologies
1st Floor, Reena Apartment, Kamakhya Nagar,
Adabari Tinali, Guwahati-781 012, Assam (India)
Phone : +91 7086-521-682,
Email : info@mageorange.com | info.mageorange@gmail.com
www.mageorange.org

Foreword

"Doubt thou the stars are fire; Doubt that the sun doth move; Doubt truth to be a liar; But never doubt I love."
~ William Shakespeare.

It's my pleasure again to have the privilege of writing the Foreword for my fiancé, my love, Carl Porten's second book of poems, titled ***Love's Longings... ...leaving hearts on my canvas...*** , a collection of love poems to treasure the priceless emotion of love forever. As Sarah Dessen describes, "There is never a time or place for true love. It happens accidentally, in a heartbeat, in a single flashing, throbbing moment" and when this happens, the soul awakens, realising, now drenched in love with all its 'longings' for love quenched by the emotional nourishment, the spiritual essence then revealing to us the true reality and reasoning of our existence. Love in its various forms, from parental love to the love of one's beloved, entails a spiritual journey of the soul that's fated to lead your footsteps home, finally to your abode of love, a day that awaits each and every soul, till eternity and beyond...

Love is an emotional experience for sure but at the same time it's undeniably true as well that it's a spiritual journey too asking a soul to experience the various colours and depths of the emotion of love. If it weren't ever for love, we might never have existed, and so is for love that we survive, thrive and exist as there's no greater nurturing power or emotion so great yet so subtle as love, as a part of nature and nurture, both as is love. John Donne, the iconic English metaphysical love poet in his 'Songs and Sonnets' category of love poems, describes love in "The Sun Rising" when he says, "Love, all alike, no season knows, nor clime, nor hours, days, months, which are the rags of time."

It's the strength and the weakness, the cycle of creation and destruction within the cyclical boundaries of which love dances till eternity that plays on life's stage. My dear mom's death made me realise all the more that love as the moon, has a very dark side, a painful side when it manifests through the initiation ceremony of grief and deep mourning, an intense phase of suffering ...as if it's a ritual of spiritual purgation that the soul experiences through the pain of love.

Love nurtures the soul when it's a blessing, an absolute bliss and is the Rock that steadies your stance, yet only after many battles would I realize, as I did, such was then, and such as is now that my mom's love was that massive Rock, never did it move, standing steadfast always and still protecting me from the ever crashing waves of life and I still have a feeling of finally returning to that Rock, to that love, my heart had always called 'home'. Carl's love for me too is my Rock, my peace 'home' now. Alfred Lord Tennyson opines, "Sweet is true love that is given in vain, and sweet is death that takes away pain." Carl made me realise my strength and it became much easier for me to accept my weaknesses, the vulnerabilities too that love naturally brings with it. Nicholas Sparks describes love in the image of the object of affection for whom the heart longs, "You are, and always have been, my dream."

After my mom's early departure from this world on the 4th of December, 2019, it became evident that my intense grieving process, my sense of understanding and idealism of what love is, would grow. Through my understanding that mere physical extinguishing of life can never defeat the power of love for love's a spiritual journey that every soul is fated to continue till eternity, a spiritual force to be reconed with, the force that will walk by our side forever, sometimes quietly, sometimes though, not so quietly, eventually I realised the true nature of love. This is where the strength comes from and no bigger strength there is, than that of the heart within us all.

The collection of soul-touching love poems each reader will find here would strike every note of the song we call life. ***Love's Longings... ...leaving hearts on my canvas...*** would make the readers hearts sing the song of life for life's but love and love's but life. Our dearest readers would love to be a part of this beautiful experience as their hearts would sing through these love struck words and the future writings of Carl. The bright gold like 'Midas touch' of godly love is more precious than gold itself, indeed, when it comes to enlivening souls as love enlightens and encompasses every breath of every life form as its essence permeates all life forms.

It's life and death, the two gates in the banquet hall of tranquil eternity, through which every love blessed soul or love deprived soul eventually will come to pass. This collection of love poetry is more of a bridge that the reader's psyche would build crossing the disconnect of realms, easing the mind back to that which is the most integral part of our world, and the most important emotion that defines it...Love as it ferries every soul across the ever unknown vastness of calm, placid waters of eternity.

I hope our dear readers, you all would experience an unforgettable journey of love as you become a part of the journey that Carl and I, we both have undertaken together to feel the bliss of making our souls journey towards the abode of love that beckons us both just as my wonderful mother's love beckoned me in her life and even now after her death, continues to inspire me. I hope dear readers you would experience an unforgettable journey of love, as you become a part of a journey that Carl and I have undertaken together to feel the bliss of discovering our souls, as we journey towards the abode of love that beckons us both,

Remembering my lovely mom's love and her idealism of love in the opening lines of the metaphysical English poet, Henry Vaughn's poem:

They are all Gone into the World of Light

"They are all gone into the world of light!
And I alone sit ling'ring here;
Their very memory is fair and bright,
And my sad thoughts doth clear.

It glows and glitters in my cloudy breast,
Like stars upon some gloomy grove,
Or those faint beams in which this hill is drest,
After the sun's remove."

I realise now, truly, in the essence of the literary meaning of 'love', how grief, loss, life are all but merely a part of the entangled web of love that traps us as ignorant, mortal beings, inspiring us to drink a sip from the eternal elixir of life that makes life worth its existence despite the heartaches and the torments that the blessed gift of life brings with it.

Suparna Ghosh
Place: Kolkata, West Bengal, India
Date: The 1st day of February, 2021

Preface

"In your light I learn how to love.
In your beauty, how to make poems.
You dance inside my chest where no-one sees you,
but sometimes I do, and that sight becomes this art."
~ Rumi.

Love's Longings... ...leaving hearts on my canvas... is a collection of emotions drawn to paper, in hopes that others can share with me feelings, all too often, left locked away, unseen and unheard. Oscar Wilde understood this so very subtle, intricate emotion of love and thus remarked wisely, "A life without it is like a sunless garden when the flowers are dead." My belief, that this very earth one day, will be built crossing bridges of hope as we drive along highways to heaven, built upon a foundation of wonderful love, a belief, I wake each day to help come true…

The philosophers of ancient Greece classified love into six categories, starting with familial love (in Greek, Storge), friendly love or platonic love (Philia), romantic love (Eros), self-love (Philautia), guest love (Xenia) and divine love (Agape).The highest form of idealistic love, Godly unconditional love is 'Agape' as The Bible too mentions. Every soul needs to seek it and strives to attain it, as the very nature of this universe seems to vibrate in tune with 'Agape' and we're just cosmic, time travellers bound by a delusional notion of three dimensional reality confined to our false sense of 'time and space'. Consciously or unconsciously, every soul is journeying to reach 'Agape', attain its peak and personify as "Agape" itself , blending with it for being eternally lost in it.

Heaven and Hell can be existent, only if we allow them and within my writings, I ask you to escape all connective reality, drawing pictures from the heart's truths, happy or sad, for sad too, is but only a small child, that faces misunderstandings as it comes towards us in hopes of the same affection given to its brother, happiness…

The art world holds an enigmatic, ethereal appeal to the human soul. The heart of art as is drawn on a canvas, is but romance on canvas as represented by the oil and the colour that brings life to a painting and the heart of art has thus long been drawn on the canvas as the heart on canvas as it expresses and shows respect to the adorable ideal of the most perfect, flawless emotion ever to exist in the universe, love.

As Helen Keller said,"The best and most beautiful things in the world cannot be seen or even touched, they must be felt with the heart."Through her words, I see a future, a future where all brothers and sisters alike, or not, are gathered, enveloped in a unity of unparalleled solidarity, ribboned with love...yes, love, where we'd all live life in a beautiful world led by compassion…

As a new author, through this collection of love poems titled, ***Love's Longings... ...leaving hearts on my canvas***... , I wish to connect my audience to the depths of the emotion of love that my own heart has experienced, sharing my very own deepest and most fragile of thoughts and emotions in hopes that you would enjoy abstractional views through my eyes, my vision in my poetry. Zelda Fitzgerald so aptly describes the emotion of love, "Nobody has ever measured, not even poets, how much the heart can hold."

Emotions and imagination…what more could one ask for, if with these two, it's possible to make one believe in a life they lived, happily ever after and the softer than silk lips wake up to a kiss from a heart and soul so pure that when two lovers' souls meet, it feels a shower of bliss...! Although mostly my poetry dives into the oceans of activism and humanitarianism, love, and only love, is the one that will always truly culture us and allow us to fly through the pinnacles of our soul's glory, none other could give, and my activism and humanitarian views are but the eventual outcome of the massive, universal emotion of love that has always been my inspiration and given me my much needed strength, especially in my deepest despair. Love is the fate of every soul, yours and mine, in the darkest moments of life helping us to strive with hope and carry on with the journey towards seeking light.

Love's my soul's pilgrimage, my spiritual journey, my soul's awakening to light and seeking it more after waking up from my dark stupor of despair that was once my soul's night until light dawned has been kind of a spiritually transformational experience for me. Love thus has never left me alone in 'the dark tunnel'. Through ***Love's Longings... ...leaving hearts on my canvas...*** my readers will be drawn to these same feelings, I felt whilst writing these poems from the deepest archives of my own heart… and soul...

The soul's yearning for a striking canvas artwork is manifested through the image of the heart drawn on such a canvas as it conjures many happy memories of days graced with love since the artwork creates an unwavering emotional connection in relation to the canvas of life, and the heart image on such a painting canvas helps our soul realise that the heart on the canvas is nothing else but its self-mirror image, painted as a heart on an oil canvas by the gentle strokes of a painter's brush. Richard Serra once said, "Drawing is a verb." Our soul self-reflects and self-connects, deeply introspects and self-retrospects its canvas journey when represented as a heart on an oil canvas as at the same time it's existential identity is complete by being a part of the canvas of life.

My heartfelt thanks to everyone that helped me make this book possible, including my publisher, many friends, my dear family…but mostly, my one and only true love, truly 'my happy ever after' for eternity and beyond...Clair as I call her (Suparna Ghosh). I truly hope you would enjoy this sentimental journey placed on paper from deep within my heart…and soul...with a timeless appeal till eternity and beyond...

"You are my heart, my life, my one and only thought."
~ Arthur Conan Doyle

Carl Porten
Place: Vancouver, British Columbia, Canada
Date: The 1st day of February, 2021

About the Book

Carl Porten's 'takes on love' is shown throughout this precious collection of his handpicked love poems giving voice to the universal emotion of love that touches every soul of each life in the universe while these poems speak volumes offering readers an enlightening insight to view love in a slightly different light.

"Life's not about waiting for storms to pass, but learning to dance with the wind at your back" ~ Carl Porten has this to say as he seeks to describe life.

It's not just an emotion for the sake of emotional connection but something bigger than that, how love becomes a way of life that includes and respects all sentient beings... as the lover grows spiritually in love with his beloved... love as it reaches out to all shines in every form radiating its light.

The readers can identify themselves to become a part of this rollercoaster emotional ride of Carl's journey of love that makes readers understand why longing for more is but an integral and undeniable part of our very existence...to reach the unfathomable depths of love as deep as the depths of love are... just as the mysteries of this universe... love's not only tender but immaculately perfect in its strength to be tender and yet still has the power to stand up to many harsh trials and tribulations of time.

The scythe of time fails to put an end to the saga of love...the earnest desire in every heart to long for love, the beloved and the divinity...all that can be reached through love. Love never perishes with all of its longings and leaves its prints on the eternal shores of the sands of time...love's saga is not about the cessation of existence but about the song of life and its existence...as love celebrates life... its existence... its enigma... because life can both be benign yet resilient too as it teaches our souls the core lessons that life offers as the universe wishes us to learn.

Love unfolds and celebrates the saga of life and its joys and sorrows. We then witness an ever-changing intricate interplay of light and shadow... the moods of life and the intensity of our longing for love makes us behold a delicately woven subtle weave of life made out of our longings for love...forever and beyond...across the dimensions of time and space until eternity and beyond...come embark on this timeless life changing journey of love's longings to experience eternity as it unfolds...love is all there is yet all else is but dust.

"You are a child of the universe,
no less than the trees and the stars;
you have a right to be here."

~ 'Desiderata' by Max Ehrmann

Contents

Foreword	3
Preface	7
Leaving Hearts On My Canvas…	17
Heart On My Sleeve…	19
What's In A Kiss?...	20
Your Piano This Night...	21
Cherished Beats Now Sound...	22
All Of "His" Light...	24
Dream With Me...	26
An Angel Appeared...	27
The Magic We Made...	29
A Spade, A Rake...	31
The Colour Of Love...	32
Once Left Out Of Reach...	34
Toy Soldiers...	36
She Searched To Find...	38
Push to be More...	40
Revealed To Me...	42
Maybe I Needed An Angel...	43
Mighty Wings...	45
My Reason To Breathe...	47
It Runs Through My Veins...	48
Remember The Moon...	50
With You By My Side...	52

Reflections Of Me... (You...)...	54
Reflections From Nowhere...	56
Reflections...	58
Your Garden...	60
The Girl Of My Dreams...	62
We've Found A Fast Love...	64
A Fool's Paradise...	66
You Never Left Me...	67
Acknowledgement	69

Leaving Hearts On My Canvas...

If yours be the voice,
then let mine be the song,
and if yours the feet walking
let mine come along.

If yours be the wind,
let mine be tall grass,
to feel soft on my lips
every time you blow past.

If yours be the wave,
let mine be the shore,
that waits with love's patience
for your crash once more,

and if yours be the height,
let then mine be the fall,
and that heart made of chalk
that rain washes from walls,

for a moment eternal
in your life this day,
'till the day comes again
every moment I'll take.

But fear not though my love
for rain can't erase,
and on walls over faint lines

again I would trace,

leaving cast through sun's light
and proud to display,
with this chalk in my hand
and this smile on my face,

and the bold red outline
from the drag of the chalk,
with you in my life
…and your heart on my wall…

~ Carl Porten

Heart On My Sleeve…

As you sleep,
I'm left to wonder,
and walk through your dreams
seeing thoughts of tomorrow,

your wishes I see
while I walk through your dreams,
that float behind beauty
that's never been seen…

…You're my queen, my ruler of heart,
and if your love should leave,
after crying and screaming
and fell to my knees,

my life here would end,
from a break in my heart,
that would make angels weep
and pull tears from the stars,

dull the shine where in heaven
the streets would fall dark,
as the saints mourn a true love
that's left torn apart…

…And is why I'd beg dear,
please never leave…
Take my hand, but be careful,

…my heart's on my sleeve…

~ Carl Porten

What's In A Kiss?…

What's in a kiss?
Let's think just a while,
is the touch of a loved one
that brings out a smile?

Is the feeling of love,
as you close your eyes,
that feeling you get
while your cheeks slowly rise.

Or is it the smile
that lays underneath,
softer than silk lips
your heart tries to reach?

-Or a book full o'memories
with pages still left,
that's placed in your hand
'till your very last breath~

~from a love that you'll feel
as your mind's blown away,
...by the arrow that Cupid
sent flying my way...

~ Carl Porten

Your Piano This Night...

None shall drapes flow,
from the painful window,
nor shall black out
the shadows of night,

nor the wind nor moonlight,
your piano this night,
to draw beauty from dawns
with each key black or white...

Left great monsters conduct,
thine ebony shine...
as the past of your touch
to leave ivory behind...

A Divine Requiem
doth set fire to hearts,
plaguing souls of the angels,
playing muse to the stars,

still the window felt pain,
still the wind blew on by,
as he listened his life,
...your piano this night...

~ Carl Porten

Cherished Beats Now Sound...

Have you ever been alone my friend!
Left trapped inside a room,
surrounded by your nightmares,
that won't let dreams come true!

Beginning at the finishin' line,
your feet can barely know,
the ground below an' how it felt
to get to where you're goin'!

Floating in an empty sky,
where nothing's left in sight,
you search an' search for what you lost,
but slowly lose the fight.

Have you ever watched a movie,
but don't know what's going on?
It's like knowin' all the words before
you ever heard the song!

It's an oasis that you find,
that's just a picture on a screen,
through a nightmare where your dreams are burned
an' fuelled by gasoline.

But this fear I burden
I will leave, before your pearly gates,
an' ask you why until I die,

then sit around an' wait,

'cause I know that angels come my Lord
an' when they do you'll see,
that I will not leave, an' will be here,
until you answer me.

So a'neath the stars before I sleep,
this cool September eve,
I'll pray you'll give the strength to me
an' all else that I'll need,

to carry on down pathways,
your grace has granted me,
an' be all I can to help this world
to mend an' fix an' heal.

What's broken that I come across,
that my two hands can bear,
but I know there will be nothing
with the strength that you've placed here,

in a chest left barely livin',
only cherished beats now sound,
from the love you placed inside my heart,
...I thought could not be found!...

~ Carl Porten

All Of "His" Light...

A little boy went one day
to watch the sunset fade away.
But this night from a'top of his peer from a hill,
he saw that the world was so broken an' ill.

As the light from the sun
slowly turned into night,
a mist rose from the ground
where the creatures would hide,

all alone in the dark
where they'd mess with your mind
but turn an' you'd see
that there's none your eyes find,

only blackness resides
where a shadow had been...
...leavin' monsters to dwell
in a darkness within...

An' that's why by God's grace,
we must thank Him in ways,
that his love reflects in you
through friends that you've made,

through angels that flew down
to be here with us,
in the form of these friendships
He gifted through love.

So don’t be afraid
when the sun doth fall down,
an’ the shadows are hidden
by blackness there now,

as there’ll always be
if you look deep inside,
the love God holds for you
...an’ all of His light.

~ Carl Porten

Dream With Me...

Peacefully as
you lay asleep,
an' I watch you there,
this promise I'll keep,

'neath all the stars
in the big night sky
I'll light your path...
Now go...now fly,

an' dream a dream
as big as the moon
then board your rocket
...you'll be there soon.

An' don't be afraid,
cause I've got your hand,
an' will never let go
at least not till we land.

An' then when your dream
is finished for sure,
wake up my dear,
an' dream with me some more...

~ Carl Porten

An Angel Appeared...

Someone please pinch me!
This must be a dream!
Lord where did she come from?
Please tell me she's real!

Did you send me an angel?
For all of my fails...
For all of my insults...
I should be in jail?

Still you come to my side
when I couldn't be taught,
when I never said thank you
for gifts that you brought,

Lord I never believed
as I shouted an' screamed,
demandin' dictatin'
the things I would need,

but you never heard me...
or as my eyes saw,
Lord you never came to me
an' knocked at my door.

How could you not Lord!
The question I'd wield,
but you left me there dyin'
in my battlefields...

An' I don't know your plan Lord,
an' won't ever ask,
why'd you do this
an' Lord why'd you do that!

For I know now that someone
far greater than me,
was settin' my pathway
an' leadin' these feet,

to a moment like this
when an' angel appeared,
an' answered the questions,
this heart used to wield...

~ Carl Porten

The Magic We Made...

I dream by your side
through night an' then day,
an' imagine to fill them
with love, joy an' play.

Each question unanswered
through quests we'll endure,
as we polish our armour
an' set off once more.

Off we go...
with our hearts on our sleeves,
each day bringin' beauty
flown in on a breeze.

An' dear when the time comes
to go different ways,
I'll look back and smile
at the memories we made-

-an' I'll wait for the day.
to be back by your side,
with a smile on my face
an' a love I can't hide.

But 'til that day my love
when I get the chance,

to hold you so close,
for just one last dance,

I'll keep dreaming dear
of our quests an' those days,
an' the love an' the joy,
...an' the magic we made.

~ Carl Porten

A Spade, A Rake...

...Then we...you and I,
will look above to watch the sky.
As stars run 'round to answer why,
the questions you ask, to those stars in the sky...

...For is it not of the same sweetness!
As from pink as from red,
both planted by the hands of God,
to give such lovely scents,

that bloom within a garden,
from Heaven's light above,
all the tools you need, a spade, a rake,
...an' His very own gardenin' gloves...

So plant within your garden,
through Dreams an' Hope an' Kind,
an' Grace that brings you here today,
...to share the Love you find...

~ Carl Porten

The Colour Of Love...

In troubled times,
when your heart isn't well,
I'll tell you a secret
that not many tell.

'Few hearts float
where this great river flows,
so pull up and listen,
...the power of rainbows.

For if love was blue
would it not be the sky,
and if love was green
the countryside!

If love was white,
would it not be the clouds!
If clear as rain...
every drip that fell down!

If love were red,
would it not be the sun,
to warm up a heart
from the heart it came from...

But love is no colour,
...single, alone...
...It's a rainbow, my liege
and more precious than gold,

‘cause colours will always,
brighten your day,
...but it’s rainbows, my friend,
that will show us the way...

~ Carl Porten

Once Left Out Of Reach...

The water was cold,
was deep, was stark,
...but we floated along,
as she sang through the dark,

as light stole a moment,
while moon floated by,
through a sky full o'stars
who all sent down their shine,

and this shimmering, glimmering
moment in time,
gifting peace to their hearts,
to their souls and minds,

their loving eyes fell
upon one moment more,
...as two hearts gently swayed,
'cross a water dance floor...

...What is Love?..
If not moments to share,
dreams that we live for,
to pull from thin air....

...For moments will pass,
but truth's to be told,
there are lots of hearts out there
that never behold,

who abandoned their child
leaving so far behind
and now so out of reach
they're no longer in sight...

...but still moment will pass,
and believe, I was one,
to leave moments behind
that will always be gone.

Always be passed,
to never again,
see that moment I missed
'cause my heart chose the pain,

chose to stand in the rain
while the sun shone out side,
not be seen within crowds
'cause I gave in to pride...

...but still moments passed,
and for those it's too late,
but I wait for the mailman now
at my front gate,

now each time he brings moments
my heart's grateful beats,
reach out for the moments,
once left out of reach...

~ Carl Porten

Toy Soldiers...

I sit here at this playground,
watching children swing...
reaching for their greatest dreams,
there's no song they can't sing.

But as they leave these playgrounds,
a vision softly sways,
an' takes them to a lonely world
where dreams no longer play

an' aspirations we once had,
while we flew within the clouds,
went up in flames, lost control,
an' crashed down to the ground.

Smouldering reminders,
of who we're supposed to be...
while we fight to release, the prisoned souls,
that died for what we need...

And why I'm here to let you know,
through everything you do,
if you need me child, I'll be right here,
and promise this to you.

My light will shine for you to see,
the beauty that can be,
in a world that seen through visions
that most hearts no longer see...

...But don’t lose hope an’ trust you’ll hear,
my call is loud an’ true
an’ anything that you can want,
is all that I will do.

With you beside me on this path,
I’ll stay forever more
an’ will fight the monsters an’ the demons,
knockin’ at the door...

I’ll end this now, an’ say goodbye
but pray my friend you’ll hear this cry.
For all I see, is all I do,
...an’ shall reflect, when I meet you...

~ Carl Porten

She Searched To Find...

I often think of photographs,
I store within my mind,
while sitting upon lonely shores,
that wash away my finds-

-I couldn't see your face that day,
I searched an' travelled far.
Pulled back the oceans, searched below,
...an' travelled past the stars.

Still your face remindin' me
through tears in every flower I see,
since the Lord did call your name,
an' took you far away from me.

God, why was I the one to pay
to sit here all alone?
Throwin' sand into an ocean ~that,
get thrown back at me as stones!

I never wanted much I'd say,
but what I couldn't find,
in a world I thought too horrible,
and scared me all the time

an' now I sit here bruised an' hurt
from all these rock hard stones,
why'd you take away the only thing
that made me feel like home?

Heaven must've needed angels,
Lord you could have told the truth..
That you yourself did call her home,
to come an' be with you,

least a reverence within my heart,
says things will turn out fine,
now I know she's looking down on me,
sat with you by your side,

makin' certain that I hear her prayers
through everything I do,
an' my work on earth reflects my Lord,
but only through your truth.

So I'll hide no more here thinkin'
that I'm sat here all alone,
an' continue what you taught me love,
from watchin' as we've grown.

For the love you gave I feel each day,
it opens up my eyes,
to feel the sunlight touch my face,
from the glory of the sky,

…an' why?

I'll promise an angel in Heaven above
who sits there by your side,
an' will fight for the Heaven, here on earth
...she searched so hard to find...

~ Carl Porten

Push to be More...

A drip lands...
lay'd to the ground,
from the red of the petal
from whence it fell down,

as the mist from the the mornin'
opened the skies,
to clear such a beauty,
an' fall on these eyes....

I will, I promise,
my vow to you,
be all that you'll need,
to make come true,

your farthest dreams
an' wildest desires,
from a love burnin' inside
that's fuelled by great fires...

a day did come,
that granted a night,
that entered my dreams
such a beautiful sight,

yet never my mind
or wildest dreams,
not one movie had played
such a beauty I'd seen...

...an’ will ever again,
for my eyes are now yours,
an’ all that I am,
...I will push to be more.

~ Carl Porten

Revealed To Me...

I pray these days,
about a love...
Sent from angels
up above!

A love so strong,
a love so true,
that no human on earth,
had ever knew...

God sent down His words,
on the wings of an angel,
to tend to a heart
left so battered an' fragile...

With band aids from Heaven,
the angel set forth,
to mend what was broken,
an' tend to my sores,

then revealed to me
right in front of my eyes,
was my Princess from heaven,
...whose love saved my life.

~ Carl Porten

Maybe I Needed An Angel...

I've been to places
my eyes haven't seen,
an' my feet have brushed pavements
where they've never been,

but the day that the earth
felt your touch on her skin
when you fell from the heavens
to help me fit in,

an' graced me with smiles
that warmed a cold heart,
that was empty, left broken,
an' fallen apart,

until you fell from heaven
an' showed me the way,
...where was dark once is lit now
like night turned to day

where were field of demons
once stood in a line,
takin' swipes at my soul
as they played with my mind, but,

now tall grass sways hand
in hand with the breeze,
takin' stage as I run
past these demons an' beasts,

an’ released,.....
like a wave crashing shore
where these demons in daylight
won’t scare me no more,

not since you fell from heaven
an’ knocked at my door,
...’cause I needed an’ angel,
a little bit more...

~ Carl Porten

Mighty Wings...

Where will I go
...today?
Where will I see!
When I go out to play?

An' what will I feel?
What will I touch?
An' what treasures will lay
past great armies I'll crush!...

Will I cross oceans?
Or climb to the top?
To view landscapes from heights
that my eyes have forgot,

or will I fly humbled
through shadows of love?
Cast by the wings
from the angels above...

Whether flying or sailing
or battling foes,
don't lose sight of your dreams,
or ever let go,

'cause without,
...we give up to fly
and lose sight of a child
and his dreams and his fight,

and his plight loses out
as he falls crashing down,
and his wings like his dreams
lay to burn on the ground...

Dreams float above,
it's where they are found...
don't be scared of the view,
or the long long way down,

but believe in a heart
that can spread mighty wings,
and would float you through currents
where God's angels sing.

Just believe in yourself,
'neath your wings looking down
and soar to find dreams,
...that some say can't be found...

~ Carl Porten

My Reason To Breathe...

I don't need hope,
or prayers or dreams
to make me believe
in anything,

and I don't need a height
to believe I can fly,
or great sails to move me
as wind passes by.

I don't need a teacher
to tell me what's right,
and I don't need a book
to show me the light,

I don't need, I don't need!
I don't need, I don't need!
...For the love you give,
is my reason to breathe...

~ Carl Porten

It Runs Through My Veins...

The sun's shining bright
then the dead of the night,
with dark rolling clouds
and bright green lightening strikes,

as the calmness before
flies out of the door,
and black clouds form a monster
a hundred feet tall,

I just stepped outside,
it's like truth hiding lies,
when your mind can't make sense
of what falls on your eyes!

And now stuck here, frozen
paralyzed,
as monsters come closer
so I close my eyes,

but still lightening strikes
and still noise from the skies,
soak through my eyelids
as cyclones collide...

...while all through my body,
it runs through my veins
so I open my eyes,
...and they're all gone again.

The sun’s shining bright,
...there’s birds flying high,
and the clouds in the sky
have all turned back to white...

~ Carl Porten

Remember The Moon...

The wind blew the tears
from sights in my eyes ,
as speed kept on reaching,
and blurry past by...

...and as I kept on falling,
from out of the sky,
...the tears from the blurry,
got left far behind...

and I watched...
fading far beyond sight
one by one disappearing,
this could not be right.

How could it be left out of sight!
And left far behind,
rule the winds that we sail 'neath
in our pond this night.

For does not the light flow!
And does not the breeze blow!
And does not the moon's shine
'cross a calm water show!

That 'til pebbles are cast,
only calmness will pass,
but when rocks cast by hands
is when mighty waves crash...

Remember the moon,
and the calm of your pond,
and find strength in still waters,
where no waves are found.

~ Carl Porten

With You By My Side...

Would you pick me up
.......if I fell!
Would you rescue me,
if I got locked in jail?

An' would you be the warm
that is given by fire,
that helps carry my load
so that I can dream higher!

Would you be the one...
...when it's dark that gives light
an' help settle my heart
to sleep better at night?

Could you be the one
as falls on these lips,
softer with passion
than Gods mornin' mist!...

...Could it be?
Is it so!
That you'd travel this far
just to help bring me home~

~I guess home's where the heart is,
an' with you by side,
all the blackness is gone
since you came with your light,

now I've found a new place,
a new life from a face,
that arrived from the heavens
to gift me God's grace.

My promise to you,
from bended knee,
is to return the love,
that you've given to me,

an' the strength
…the fact that my life,
will always be better,
with you by my side...

~ Carl Porten

Reflections Of Me...
(You...)...

I've been losing sleep
an' sitting at night,
with my eyes to the stars
an' with wishes to find.

Yet my gaze from dreams,
an' wishes on stars,
...all I find's my reflection
alone in the dark...

But tonight I'll look hard.
Tonight I'll lose sleep,
as I search for a promise
I promised to keep...

A promise to me
that I made as a child,
long before life had taken
an' rewrote my life.

I've been losing sleep
an' sitting at night,
...but now my reflection helps
dreams come to life,

helps wishes come true,
from a heart I set free...
...I'm so glad I made friends with,
reflections of me...

~ Carl Porten

Reflections From Nowhere...

"Take to depth,
and from within you,
from within...pull, for sweetness,

would thee ask,
...for closing a statement,
whilst raised a skull?..."

...These pictures here,
they still make me weep.
Is it real what I see?
Or just dreams as I sleep?

Is it as I reach out...
...something I find?
Or just pictures through sleep
that float softly on by?

Is it all of the places
that I've ever been?
...Or nowhere at all,
and no place that I've seen?

Will not it lay tamed?
As my eyes again fall,
over sights never owned
yet my mind owns them all...

How Cruel can be!
As they fall upon me,
more reflections from nowhere
that no one else sees...

I open my eyes,
under crackling skies,
...in the real world the sky's blue...
why can't my eyes disguise?

The colour of light
isn't bright, isn't white,
but is darker than shadows,
in blackness of night.

It's a fool's paradise,
the cross...the nails,
and you're already there,
...you just don't feel the pain!...

~ Carl Porten

Reflections...

Do you love me?...
No...do you really love me?
For I look into your eyes
but cannot really see...

...Do you love me?...
...How can't my heart know?
You've been here all along
an' I thought you'd have shown...

...but doubts lay inside
as I gaze though these eyes,
to a mirrored reflection
you've hid well behind~

~all your life...
an' I'm sorry to say,
but I loved you much more
in your childhood days,

where innocence bloomed
in a fearless heart.
But once you grew up child,
...my dear where's your heart?

An' why now those tears,
filled with such pain?
Child what happened that Sadness
kicked Happy from reign?...

There are rules in life,
an' things we must do,
pray listen these words
or your dream won't come true~

~don't forget who you were
while you ran with your friends,
fighting pirates an' monsters
that lived past lands ends,

an' never forget
to give love from a child,
...who's hid long in this mirror,
in front of my eyes...

~ Carl Porten

Your Garden...

Will you be ready,
when angels come?
...The ones we deny
'cause a monster's more fun...

These are not aliens,
monsters or Gods,
but a sadness we live
from a past we forgot.

Planted gardens
that see no sun,
where the warmth of its love
can't be felt by someone.

This is a crime,
a soul left denied...
Is it grace! Is it fear!
That took what was inside?

That stole existence,
now looking above,
at the body you had
that now lays there no good...

...To try is all...
but try we should,
... for a heart's outside waiting,
for your garden's love!...

~ Carl Porten

The Girl Of My Dreams...

You're the girl of my dreams,
in my sky you're a star,
your'e the wheels on my truck
which without won't go far.

You're the light in my life,
the surprise in my box,
you're my old favourite toy
that I thought I had forgot.

You're the view from the hilltop
that captured my heart,
you're the rays from the sun,
you're the wishes on stars.

You're the wind in the air,
you're the sweet scent of love,
...but you breath all this life,
yet still feel bereft of...

But bereft of what dear
for a heart such as yours,
that can change swaying tides
and so very much more!...

I've seen time stand still,
and I've flown up above,
I've conquered the depths,
and climbed higher than love,

been to places past never,
seen sights beyond words,
felt the beauty of nothing,
heard what can't be heard...

but never before dear,
or futures do see,
have brought into my heart,
what your heart brings to me...

So again I'll take breath
from the wind that you are,
and again I'll make wishes
on bright shining stars,

and again I'll dive down
into depths far below,
and climb mountains for sunsets
to see where we'll go,

...And we'll go...

~ Carl Porten

We've Found A Fast Love...

We've found a fast love,
can we drive forever?
And follow our dreams,

and never ever get enough,
'cause we'll follow all the signs
that'll make it feel real.

And babe when we get there,
we can build a tomorrow
that no one else knew,

'cause it's our dream in our heart
and the love that we share
will make it come true.

Cold December will remind us,
when the chill of the night surrounds us
and the snow will melt from our love
when the fire that unites us,

burns bright to find a stage where
we can dance at night alone there,
and time will slow right down dear,

when I whisper into your ear...

I've found a fast love,
and I'll drive to forever,
and follow my dreams,

and I’ll never get enough,
‘cause I’ll follow all the signs
that’ll make it feel real...

~ Carl Porten

A Fool's Paradise...

..."A Fool's Paradise..."...
...read the words 'bove the frame,
of a doorway that hangs now
from old rusty nails...

...in a world where our dreams,
are stopped before started,
once ones we looked up to
now sit broken hearted...

...Through whispered vocations
we've bartered to buy,
in a lifetime of sadness
as happy floats by, now

'neath shimmering blinkin',
of rouge lit nights,
shows clear a sign readin'...
..."A Fools Paradise..."

~ Carl Porten

You Never Left Me...

...What Lord did I do?..
Please tell me in a dream,
to not bring me a princess
but gift me a queen! Lord...

...I thought all these years
as I screamed from below,
up to skies past the clouds
to the place you call home,

I cussed an' cursed,
an' called you for worth,
that I thought in my mind
was more than you deserved,

Still you stayed,
an' just let me be,
never shouted or screamed,
but just walked beside me...

...Thank you Lord for this gift,
that your heart hath graced me,
please forgive this once boy,
...for not seeing what I see.

~ Carl Porten

Acknowledgement

Cover Page Image has been taken from:

https://pixabay.com/illustrations/murals-children-drawing-paint-1320739/

www.ingramcontent.com/pod-product-compliance
Lightning Source LLC
Chambersburg PA
CBHW050024170726
48282CB00025B/543
* 9 7 8 8 1 9 4 9 4 5 1 7 8 *